THE OFFICIAL
Wolves
ANNUAL 2017

Written by Paul Berry

Designed by Abbie Groom,
Synaxis Design Consultancy Ltd

A Grange Publication

© 2016. Published by Grange Communications Ltd., Edinburgh, under licence from Wolverhampton Wanderers Football Club. Printed in the EU.

Every effort has been made to ensure the accuracy of information within this publication but the publishers cannot be held responsible for any errors or omissions. Views expressed are those of the author and do not necessarily represent those of the publishers or the football club. All rights reserved.

Photographs © AMA Sport Agency, Sam Bagnall, Dave Bagnall, Matt Ashton, Stuart Manley, Shaun Mallen (SM2 Studio), James Baylis, Action Images, Shutterstock and the Wolves Archive.

ISBN: 978-1-911287-18-6

Contents

WELCOME, WALTER!

Walter Zenga didn't have too long to get to work after being appointed as Wolves Head Coach in the summer of 2016.

He was appointed seven days before the season, and started training five days before the Sky Bet Championship campaign kicked off at Rotherham.

Zenga arrived at Molineux with a wealth of experience in both playing and coaching, arguably one of world football's greatest goalkeepers back in the day, and having won titles with Steaua Bucharest and Red Star Belgrade from the dugout.

Here are a few photos and facts about the Italian whom Wolves fans were hoping would bring success back to Molineux in pursuit of the Premier League.

Walter spent the majority of his playing career with Inter Milan, but also played for Sampdoria. He once played a UEFA Cup tie for Inter Milan at Villa Park against an Aston Villa side including a certain Tony Daley!

Walter was one of Italian football's greats as a goalkeeper, and was regarded as one of the world's best as well. He kept five clean sheets in the 1990 World Cup, and was in goal in the Italy/England third place play-off in which Steve Bull was an unused substitute for the Three Lions.

Among his coaching/managerial achievements prior to joining Wolves, Zenga won the domestic double in the 2005/06 season in Serbia with Red Star Belgrade.

Having been announced as new Head Coach in the morning of Wolves' final pre-season friendly with Swansea, Zenga then made it to Molineux to see the stadium and introduce himself to players and staff for the first time.

Two new members of staff also arrived with Walter at Wolves – assistant head coach Stefano Cusin, who had worked with him previously, and Team General Manager Andrea Butti, formerly Press and Team Manager at Inter Milan and Assistant Technical Director at Monaco.

Walter told the press conference at his official 'unveiling' at Molineux how proud and honoured he was to have landed the position. "I will do everything to give my heart to this amazing club," he said.

Walter got straight to work on the training ground to get his approach and ideas across to the squad. Among the aims were to transmit his passion and enthusiasm to the players.

A rousing comeback from his players capped an emotional first game in charge, notably for the reception received from supporters. "I am a man of 56 years old, but the reaction I got from our fans today made me emotional," said Zenga.

Danny Batth kept the captaincy with the arrival of the new Head Coach and the pair shared a rousing post-match moment after the comeback for a point on the opening day.

Walter endeared himself to fans fairly swiftly with his passionate approach. They sang his name before, during, and after the opening game of the season at Rotherham.

AUGUST

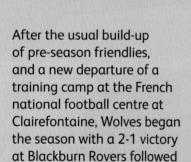

After the usual build-up of pre-season friendlies, and a new departure of a training camp at the French national football centre at Clairefontaine, Wolves began the season with a 2-1 victory at Blackburn Rovers followed by a 1-1 draw with Hull City.

Defeats against QPR and Cardiff dented any early optimism before a late comeback victory against Charlton.

There was an element of the changing of the guard with Bakary Sako having departed, Nouha Dicko unfortunately suffering a long-term injury, and double Player of the Year winner Richard Stearman moving to Fulham.

Several new faces had arrived, including Conor Coady, Jed Wallace, Nathan Byrne and loan trio Emi Martinez, Sheyi Ojo and Adam Le Fondre.

SEPTEMBER

Not the best of months, until the final game which brought a superb 3-0 win at Fulham, coming the day after it had been announced that Steve Morgan was ready to listen to offers from potential new owners.

Up until then it had been a difficult month, a defeat at lowly Bolton followed by draws with Brighton and a Preston team reduced to nine men.

Wolves also went out of the Capital One Cup, beaten convincingly at Middlesbrough having progressed through with a win against Barnet the previous month.

OCTOBER

Another mixed month, begun in fine style with an identical result to that which finished September, a 3-0 victory, this time at home to Huddersfield Town.

But then came three successive defeats by two-goal margins with a total of nine goals conceded to Derby, Brentford and Middlesbrough.

Yet the month was finished off with what was to prove one of the happiest awaydays of the campaign, a convincing 2-0 success at Midlands rivals Birmingham City.

NOVEMBER

Just three points from four games in November as, for a second successive season, Wolves found this month particularly tough.

A hugely disappointing defeat at Bristol City was followed by draws with Burnley and Ipswich who were both flying high towards the top end of the Sky Bet Championship.

But there was perhaps a greater sense of frustration on the final weekend of November, as Wolves were unable to break down a stubborn MK Dons side in a goalless draw at Molineux.

DECEMBER

The usual busy festive schedule, and, after a hard-fought win at Rotherham and draw against Nottingham Forest, there followed defeats against Leeds and Sheffield Wednesday.

The latter was particularly heavy, and particularly disappointing, and left Wolves on a worrying sequence of only two wins from 12.

At that stage the need for character was paramount, and so it proved, the year coming to an end with successive clean sheets, and victories, against Reading and Charlton respectively.

JANUARY

Two successive league wins turned into four in very different circumstances, a battling 1-0 win at Brighton on New Year's Day and then a rollercoaster 3-2 victory at home to Fulham at Molineux.

But a fifth success proved a bridge too far as Cardiff conquered to complete a league double which was followed up by a 1-1 stalemate at Queens Park Rangers.

Wolves' stay in the Emirates FA Cup was brief and despite putting up a decent showing on their last ever visit to West Ham's Boleyn Ground, they were undone by a late goal from Nikica Jelavic.

Player movement saw top scorer Benik Afobe depart for AFC Bournemouth, and Scott Golbourne for Bristol City, with Mike Williamson, Joe Mason and Michal Zyro checking in.

FEBRUARY

Not a good month for Wolves, as a run of two without a win became seven until George Saville popped up with a clinical and match-winning brace to defeat promotion-chasing Derby County at Molineux.

Draws against Bolton and Reading could, and possibly should, have been wins, as a 2-0 lead was let slip against the Trotters and chances squandered in a goalless draw at the Royals.

But there wasn't too much to shout about in the following three matches prior to Derby, defeats at the hands of Preston, Huddersfield and Brentford.

MARCH

A long old Friday night trip to Middlesbrough, one of many fixtures moved during the season for live coverage by Sky Sports, ended in a 2-1 defeat when a late goal proved only a consolation.

But an even later goal at home to Bristol City was far more beneficial, Matt Doherty in the fourth minute of added time sealing victory by the same scoreline.

Hard fought draws with Birmingham and Burnley followed, the latter thanks to another hugely acclaimed late show, a powerful header from skipper Danny Batth.

APRIL

The unbeaten run stretched to seven games in early April, goalless draws at home either side of a 2-1 win at MK Dons which came at a cost with another severe injury, this time to Michal Zyro.

And this came after a similar injury had curtailed Jordan Graham's electric start to his Wolves career back in January.

By contrast, Jack Price's close range winner at Stadium MK was one of the season's memorable moments, but successive 2-1 defeats at Hull and Leeds were less so.

Another 0-0 draw at home against Rotherham set an unwanted club record of four successive goalless Molineux stalemates, before the month finished with another draw, 1-1 away at Nottingham Forest.

Just one game in May, the visit of play-off bound Sheffield Wednesday, who made many changes to their starting line-up ahead of their battle with Brighton.

Amid a superb atmosphere at Molineux, and in front of a crowd of 25,488, Wolves ran out 2-1 winners to finish up 14th in the Sky Bet Championship table, a rare mid-table finish in recent seasons.

The annual Player of the Year awards took place three days later, with Matt Doherty landing a hat trick- Supporters' and Players' accolades and Goal of the Season for his long range strike against Fulham.

Wolves & England

Wolves defenders Dominic Iorfa and Kortney Hause have emerged as excellent prospects in recent years, not only playing regularly for their club but also England junior teams up to and including the Under-21s.

The summer of 2016 was a particularly successful one for the defensive duo, both playing key roles as England Under-21s won the illustrious Toulon tournament in France.

And during one of Dominic's call-ups with the Under-21s, he was drafted in to train with the England senior team at St George's Park, Wayne Rooney and all!

WHO'S THE DADI?

Jon Dadi Bodvarsson, that's who.

The powerful Icelandic striker joined Wolves from Kaiserslautern off the back of an impressive European Championship.

Bodvarsson scored in Iceland's group win against Austria and was part of the team which defeated England en route to the quarter finals.

His first appearance for Wolves was equally memorable.

On the day he became the club's 1000th league player, he notched a superb late equaliser against Rotherham, then celebrated post match with the 'Viking Clap' made famous by his countrymen during the Euros.

DOC'S BEST

The 2015/16 season was a good one for Matt Doherty who not only claimed a hat-trick of awards: Fans' and Players' Player of the Year and Goal of the Season, but also landed his first senior international call-up with the Republic of Ireland.

BEST MUSICAL TASTES

"I'd say Kortney Hause. He's got some decent hip hop going on. He doesn't know his reggae like I do though."

THE HAPPIEST

"Conor Coady. Without a doubt. He is so happy it actually annoys me. He is so positive. If anyone tells any sort of joke, even if it's not that good, he laughs like it is the funniest joke he has ever heard! It can be so annoying. I am on his case that he laughs so much at jokes. Sometimes things just aren't that funny, and just a little laugh will do."

MOST INTELLIGENT

"Apart from myself? The most intelligent is Eddo (Dave Edwards). I have seen him on Sky Sports and other TV and he talks a great game. He convinces me with everything that he says. I end up agreeing with him and thinking 'yes, he must be right'. He is one of the cleverer ones in our dressing room that's for sure."

BEST BANTER

"Jed Wallace is quite funny. He makes me laugh quite a bit.

It was his first season last season so he was new in the dressing room and probably still feels he needs to make a good impression on the boys. So he does over-do it sometimes. He gets me the odd time though."

BEST CLOTHES

"James Henry dresses in his best gear every day, although he wears his jeans very high. I'll go with James, it might cheer him up."

BEST DANCER

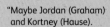

"Maybe Jordan (Graham) and Kortney (Hause).

I'm not sure many of us are dancers but those two have got some rhythm."

THE QUIETEST

"Joe Mason. He's chilled. Comes in, gets the job done, and goes home."

WHAT WOULD THE REST OF THE SQUAD SAY ABOUT MATT DOHERTY?

AND WORST

But what does Doc think of his Wolves team-mates?
The Wolves Annual just had to find out as we asked the versatile
defender about the good and bad in the Wolves dressing room!

THE ⚠ LOUDEST

"Jed Wallace. As I said earlier, he is still trying to make that impression. Trying to give the impression he is comfortable around the boys. But deep down he is still on edge and in that honeymoon period."

WORST ⚠ BANTER

"He has left us now but Bjorn Sigurdarson was with us for a few years and he had some really dry banter. Sometimes it was funny. But I'm not sure any of us knew what he did in his spare time. I'm probably being harsh, because he did make me laugh, but I'll go for Bjorn."

WORST ⚠ MUSICAL TASTES

"Danny Batth. He just listens to pure noise. It's truly horrific.

Although if the lads listened to the music I've got on my phone I would have serious problems in this category. There is a lot of soft stuff with me: piano music, classical stuff."

WORST ⚠ CLOTHES

"Another who has left the club now but it has to be Aaron McCarey. You could have gone into our dressing room on any day and just looked at his peg and you would know exactly what I meant. He was the worst by far. Shambolic is the word."

THE ⚠ GRUMPIEST

"James Henry. He is just never wrong. And that can make him grumpy if people don't agree with him. You can't win an argument against him, no matter what. He gets sarcastic very quickly too."

"That I am different. Some might say unique."

WORST ⚠ DANCER

"It's Aaron (McCarey) again. Without a doubt. I've got more rhythm standing still than he has got when he tries to dance. It's quite cringey to watch."

LEAST ⚠ INTELLIGENT

"George Saville. By miles. Although he is very good with numbers. He is so thick otherwise. I have told him that so I am not speaking out of turn. And he admits it as well: no problem. But with maths he is very clever. Fair play to him."

Wolfie's FUN PAGE

COLOUR ME IN! ↓

Answers on page **61**

Getting Shirty!

Wolfie has been drawing Wolves shirts but all of the names of the players have been scrambled! Can you work out which players' names have been scrambled?

CODKI

LAISLEV

DEDRAWS

Crest Jumble

Wolfie has mixed up four crests of other teams in our league for the 2016/17 Season! Do you know to which teams the crests belong?

1882

B

Did you know?

Greenland aren't able to join FIFA because there's not enough grass to grow good quality pitches.

Spot the Difference

Can you find the 5 differences between the two pictures below?

Puzzled!

Can you find the puzzle piece that has been removed from Wolfie's picture?

Monster Wordsearch

This year's Monster Wordsearch focuses on those through history who have had the privilege of managing Wolves.

Up until the end of the 2015/16 season, there have been 28 permanent managers/ head coaches of the club.

Can you find all of their surnames as shown below?

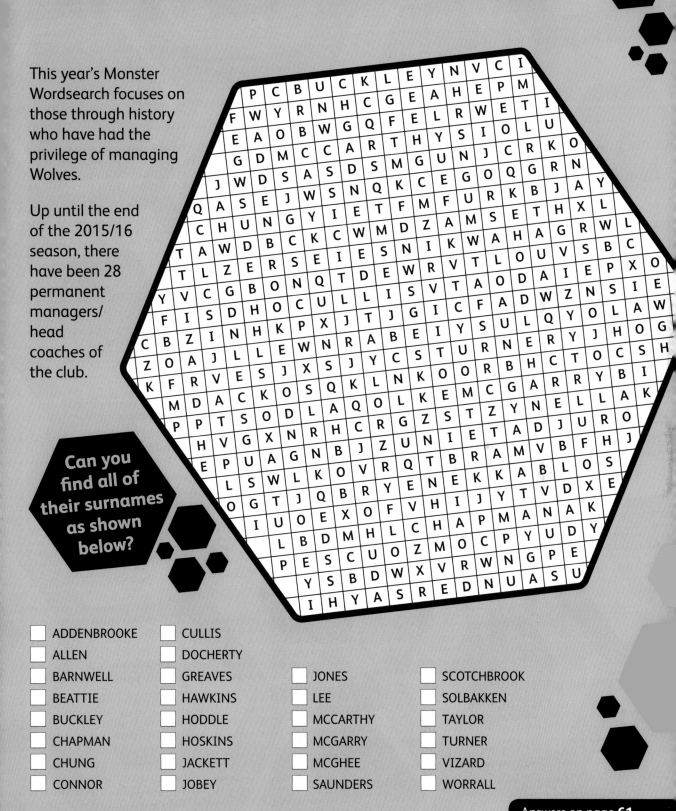

- [ ] ADDENBROOKE
- [ ] ALLEN
- [ ] BARNWELL
- [ ] BEATTIE
- [ ] BUCKLEY
- [ ] CHAPMAN
- [ ] CHUNG
- [ ] CONNOR
- [ ] CULLIS
- [ ] DOCHERTY
- [ ] GREAVES
- [ ] HAWKINS
- [ ] HODDLE
- [ ] HOSKINS
- [ ] JACKETT
- [ ] JOBEY
- [ ] JONES
- [ ] LEE
- [ ] MCCARTHY
- [ ] MCGARRY
- [ ] MCGHEE
- [ ] SAUNDERS
- [ ] SCOTCHBROOK
- [ ] SOLBAKKEN
- [ ] TAYLOR
- [ ] TURNER
- [ ] VIZARD
- [ ] WORRALL

(Please note that caretaker managers are not included).

Answers on page **61**

23

NOUHA'S TOP FIVE

Losing Nouha Dicko to injury at the start of the 2015/16 season was a massive blow, both for the player himself and for Wolves. The livewire striker is a pocket rocket, full of power and pace, and has already scored some impressive goals in a career which has much more to come.

We asked Nouha to give us his top five goals in his own words, as at the end of that 2015/16 campaign. He duly obliged and also put them in order!

BLACKPOOL
v Doncaster
(February 2012)

"Not a particularly beautiful goal but for me it was all about the meaning of it. It was my first league goal in English football, which came for Blackpool against Doncaster.

It was a tap-in but it was my first so it meant a lot to me. It was our third goal in a 3-1 win."

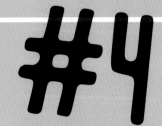

ROTHERHAM
v Wolves
(December 2013)

Picture courtesy of Jim Brailsford/Rotherham FC

"Wolves fans won't be happy but this was a goal for Rotherham against Wolves. I scored with my chest! It was a great game with a really good atmosphere and things were going well for me at the time.

I played the ball wide to Ben Pringle and he crossed it and I finished it off with my chest. It was a different goal and that is why it is one of my favourites. And maybe it helped me get to Wolves as I signed not long afterwards!"

#3

WOLVES
v Leeds
(April 2015)

"It was the second goal I scored in a really good game against Leeds, which ended in a 4-3 win. It came from a good ball in behind the defence from Bakary (Sako). It was the sort of pass that I like to get on the end of. And then I hit the ball first time to beat the keeper. I knew I could have had another touch but that is why it is one of my favourites. Because other players might have taken another touch. It made for a beautiful goal and even now when I watch it I am very happy about it."

#2

WOLVES
v Port Vale
(March 2014)

"This goal came from another ball from Bakary in behind. It was a longer ball, maybe a 30 to 40 yards pass. It left me fighting against two defenders. I managed to get my body in there, and ended up being one of the goals I like to score, using power and pace and a bit of skill. I managed to flick the ball over the defender and was strong when he tried to push me. And then I scored with a half volley with my left foot which doesn't happen a lot!"

#1

BLACKPOOL
v Hull City
(October 2012)

"This goal was an overhead kick and is the best goal I have scored yet. I can still see myself now scoring it - it was a late winner too for a 3-2 win with only a few minutes to go so the feeling was amazing.
A cross came in and it fell to me. I chested the ball and then finished into the net with an acrobatic overhead kick.

As a kid they are the goals I always wanted to score. I can still see myself practising overhead kicks and landing on my Mum's bed when I was young! I hope Wolves fans can forgive me choosing this as my number one. It just spurs me on to score an overhead kick for Wolves which can take over at the top!"

Wolves

Jeff Shi

WOLVERHAMPTON
WANDERERS FC

We Believe in You

WELCOME
FOSUN 复星

It was, as departing Chief Executive Jez Moxey described, a 'momentous day' for Wolves shortly before the 2016/17 season as major Chinese investors Fosun Group took ownership of the club from Steve Morgan.

Wolves director Jeff Shi, pictured above, attended a press conference with Jez, not to mention met the Club's legendary record goalscorer and Vice-President Steve Bull.

Then, hundreds of fans gathered outside Molineux during the media conference to wish Jeff well as Wolves aimed to move into an exciting new era.

Guo Guangchang, chairman of Fosun, pictured right with Wolves Managing Director Laurie Dalrymple, then came along to Molineux and Compton Park on the

first day of the season to make his first visit to the club, after which he travelled to Rotherham to enjoy the exciting curtain-raiser to the new campaign as Jon

Dadi Bodvarsson's equaliser secured a 2-2 draw.

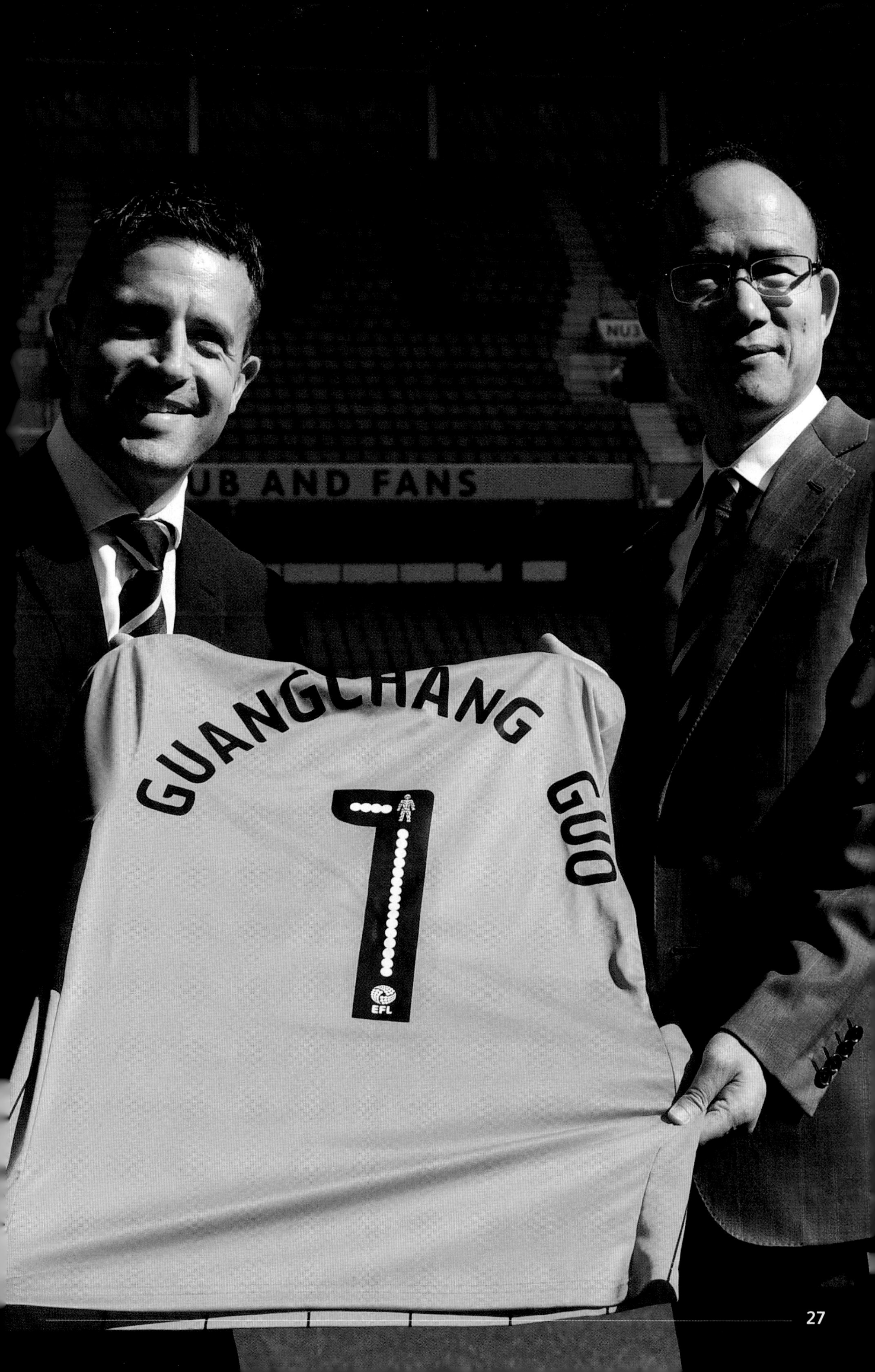
UB AND FANS
GUANGCHANG GUO
1
EFL

Portuguese magician
Joao Teixeira.

WELCOME THE NEW BOYS!

There was an all-changed Wolves squad at the start of the 2016/17 season with a flurry of new senior arrivals to try and boost the club's chances of a successful campaign. **So here we pay a pictorial tribute to the Molineux New Boys... Including one who isn't quite as new as the rest!**

Jon Dadi Bodvarsson joined Wolves, as did the Icelandic Viking Thunder Clap!

Highly-rated Manchester United defender **Cameron Borthwick-Jackson** is to spend a season at Molineux.

A Prince among Wolves as **Prince Oniangue** checks in!

Ola John all smiles after completing his loan from Benfica.

Helder Costa is hoping to bring some wing wizardry to Wolves.

Portuguese international forward **Ivan Cavaleiro** joined Wolves on a five year contract from AS Monaco

Powerful striker **Paul Gladon** made the move to Molineux from Dutch side Heracles Almelo.

Defender **Silvio** arrived from Atletico Madrid.

Keeper **Andy Lonergan** made the move from Fulham.

Richard Stearman - the Wanderer returns on a season-long loan!

The highly-rated **Romain Saiss** arrived from Angers, where he was Player of the Year.

Pre-season is always a time for the players to get themselves fit and in tip-top condition for the new season. But the **Wolves Annual** decided to take a more humorous look at a selection of pre-season photos from club photographer Sam Bagnall.

BACK TO SCHOOL!

Schooldays are the best days of your life, surely? Well apart maybe from being a footballer.

Let's combine the two – and ask a load of footballers about their favourite school memory.

A few of the Wolves lads gave us their answers!

ETHAN EBANKS-LANDELL

"Watching kids fighting (but you shouldn't do that kids!)"

MATT DOHERTY

"Being at a school with girls"

MICHAL ZYRO

"Getting outside at play time"

CONOR COADY

"Playing footy with your mates"

JED WALLACE

"Football games – against our local rivals"

DAVE EDWARDS

"A geography field trip – to Alton Towers!"

CARL
IKEME

"PE lessons"

ANDY
LONERGAN

"Playing football
at break"

JACK
PRICE

"Winning the
Year 11
Cup Final"

DANNY
BATTH

"Living just down the road
(so easy to get to!)"

JOE
MASON

"Going to
Disneyland Paris"

JORDAN
GRAHAM

"Being a
showman"

KORTNEY
HAUSE

"Earning pocket
money selling
stuff (sweets
etc!)"

JAMES
HENRY

"Not having any
responsibilities"

MIKE
WILLIAMSON

"Representing the
school at athletics
(long jump)"

GETTING TO KNOW YOU

Not only are Kortney Hause and Jordan Graham very good mates off the pitch, at times they have been house-mates, with both players at Wolves away from their London and Coventry roots respectively. So how well do they know each other? We asked each of them a series of questions about the other, to answer that very question!

JORDAN
ON KORTNEY

WHAT IS KORTNEY'S FAVOURITE TV SHOW?

(A) Prison Break
(B) House
(C) Homeland

JG: Prison Break. All day.

CORRECT 1/1

WHAT IS KORTNEY'S FAVOURITE FILM?

(A) Taken
(B) Scarface
(C) Big Momma's House

JG: I know he likes Taken and he likes Scarface. Tough one. I'll go Taken.

AHH NO! 1/2

WHO IS KORTNEY'S FAVOURITE MUSICAL ARTIST?

(A) Drake
(B) Future
(C) The Housemartins

JG: Drake. Always!
(the two start singing)

CORRECT 2/3

WHO IS KORTNEY'S SPORTING HERO?

(A) Muhammad Ali
(B) Ronaldinho
(C) John Terry

JG: Muhammad Ali.

CORRECT 3/4

WHAT IS KORTNEY'S MOST ANNOYING HABIT?

(A) Bad Instagram photos
(B) Always late
(C) I don't have any!

JG: Always late!
KH: I said I don't have any!
JG: I thought you might, but you are always late!

WRONG 3/5

WHAT IS KORTNEY'S FAVOURITE ITEM OF CLOTHING?

(A) Louboutins Shoes
(B) Superman boxer shorts
(C) Chain

JG: Louboutins. Has to be.

CORRECT 4/6

WHAT MEAL WOULD KORTNEY COOK?

(A) Spaghetti Bolognaise
(B) Beans On Toast
(C) Chicken Wraps

JG: Chicken wraps! They are decent to be fair.

YES 5/7

WHAT MAKES KORTNEY SCARED?

(A) Spiders
(B) Injections
(C) Horror Films

JG: Horror films.
KH: Yes he made me watch a film once and didn't say it was a horror film. Then I started hearing some noises in the night after!

CORRECT 6/8

WHAT IS KORTNEY'S FAVOURITE TRACK?

(A) Our House by Madness
(B) House is a feeling by Todd Terry
(C) Scholarships By Drake And Future

JG: Scholarships.
(they are singing again!)

CORRECT 7/9

WHAT IS KORTNEY'S FAVOURITE SAYING?

(A) You're Nicked Mate
(B) Leave it yeh
(C) Dench

JG: Yeh yeh yeh yeh you're nicked mate!
(we didn't dare ask)

CORRECT 8/10

KORTNEY
ON JORDAN

WHAT IS JORDAN'S FAVOURITE TV SHOW?

(A) Graham Norton
(B) Take Me Out
(C) Coronation Street

KH: Erm. I'll go with Take Me Out.

CORRECT 1/1

WHAT IS JORDAN'S FAVOURITE FILM?

(A) The Hangover
(B) Shawshank Redemption
(C) Law Abiding Citizen

KH: Law Abiding Citizen.

CLOSE! 1/2

WHO IS JORDAN'S FAVOURITE MUSICAL ARTIST?

(A) Lil Wayne
(B) Jaki Graham
(C) Jordan Knight

KH: Lil Wayne. Easy!

CORRECT 2/3

WHO IS JORDAN'S SPORTING HERO?

(A) Dominic Iorfa
(B) Lionel Messi
(C) Cristiano Ronaldo

JG: You knowwwww!
KH: Yes. Ronaldo!

CORRECT 3/4

WHAT IS JORDAN'S MOST ANNOYING HABIT?

(A) Talking too much
(B) Playing music too loud
(C) Sleeping too much

JG: Could probably say all three of them!
KH: I'll go for the talking one.

GOOD CHOICE 4/5

WHAT IS JORDAN'S FAVOURITE ITEM OF CLOTHING?

(A) Louboutins Shoes
(B) Louis Vuitton bag
(C) Baseball cap

KH: The Loubs.

CORRECT 5/6

WHAT MEAL WOULD JORDAN COOK?

(A) Golden Grahams
(B) Salmon
(C) Chicken pasta asparagus in white wine sauce

KH: The chicken.

CORRECT 6/7

WHAT MAKES JORDAN SCARED?

(A) Carl Ikeme
(B) When Jed Wallace gets the ball
(C) Heights

(Amid much laughter)
KH: When Jed gets the ball and starts legging it!

CORRECT 7/8

WHAT IS JORDAN'S FAVOURITE TRACK?

(A) Thank me Later by Drake
(B) The Birdie Song
(C) Monster by Chris Budden

KH: Monster by Chris Budden.
(they are singing again!)

INDEED 8/9

WHAT IS JORDAN'S FAVOURITE SAYING?

(A) Ya Mean
(B) Golden Graham
(C) Amazeballs

KH: Ha ha! It's Ya Mean.

CORRECT YA MEAN 9/10

VERDICT

A combined score of 17/20, or 85%, which is decent in anybody's books! Clearly Jordan and Kortney know a fair bit about each other which explains how well they get on off the pitch.

Good work gents! Ya Mean!

BEHIND
THE
SCENES!

Chances are if you've seen a programme cover or new kit picture from Wolves last season, then it was photographed and produced by SM2 Studio.

It is serious stuff, but can also be fun! As getting the players to relax as much as possible always brings about the best pictures.

Here are a few of the unseen photos from the last year's shoots.

DESERT ISLAND JED

Jed Wallace is one of the liveliest characters in the Wolves dressing room, always heavily involved in the jokes and the banter. But what would he be like if he was packed off to a desert island without any home comforts or people to talk to? Well we might let him have a few luxury items.

Here's what he would choose:

CD

"What am I listening to at the moment? I'd go with *So Far Gone* by Drake. That was one of his first albums. I actually like a lot of different music to be honest. I could go Drake, 50 Cent, My Chemical Romance in the space of two minutes. It depends on the mood I am in. When the sun is out (as I hope it will be on this island) I tend to listen to a bit more hip hop or R&B."

BOOK

"I read a lot of autobiographies. Over the summer I read Tim Cahill and Mike Tyson. Different books obviously. The previous summer I remember reading Gary Neville's book, and Craig Bellamy's. I like reading about people who have been successful and how they got to being there. Real-life stuff."

FILM

"*How To Train Your Dragon*. That is right up there for me. The main dragon is called Toothless. Me and James Henry love kids' films. We sat down to watch Inside Out when it came out on DVD. I love *The Lion King* as well, *Big Hero 6*, but *How To Train Your Dragon* takes it."

COMEDIAN

"Lee Evans. The comedian rather than our midfielder. I think he's brilliant. Although I think he'd properly get a bit annoying if I was in his company all the time. I used to like Frankie Boyle on *Mock the Week* but then think he got a bit too extreme with his views. It seemed to go down the politics route which I don't understand and I don't really like talking about stuff I don't understand."

FAMOUS PERSON

"I'd go for someone who has inspired me as I reckon I would enjoy hanging around with them. Muhammad Ali or David Beckham. Arnold Schwarzenegger. Someone who has done loads of interesting things that I could learn from"

CHILDHOOD MEMORY

"Tearing around the place with my mates. I had a field outside my house at the back of my garden and in the school holidays, from 8 o'clock in the morning until it went dark we would be out there, mainly playing football. Turned up bikes for goalposts."

FOOD

"I love food, I am really big on food. So what couldn't I live without? Nando's and sushi if I can have two. And Italian food, I love Italian food. OK then if I have to pick one, I will go for sushi."

A PIECE OF ADVICE

"Something from my Dad. He always said that in football to do 90 per cent of what the manager tells you to do, and 10 per cent of your own, and the things that have helped you become a professional footballer. So always listen to people that know what they are talking about, but also add in that five or ten per cent that makes you the person and the player you are."

TEAM-MATE YOU WOULDN'T TAKE

"Danny Batth and Carl Ikeme. Too much muscle. It wouldn't be good for my self-morale to be looking at their bodies every day. Definitely not James Henry. Too negative. And if there was any food on the island he would eat it all for himself."

TEAM-MATE

"Maybe Jordan Graham, who I constantly have a good laugh with. But actually do you know who I would take? Emi Martinez, who was with us on loan last season. He is an all-round good guy and he is from Argentina so he might know a bit about jungles and stuff. He could help us escape."

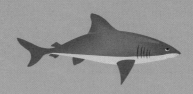

Wolves Wishes

The 2015/16 season saw another series of 'Wolves Wishes' granted, where supporters nominate other supporters to receive a special Wolves-related surprise.

These generally feature a meeting with a current or former player and some form of Wolves treat.

On these two pages are some photos from the Wishes which have taken place over the last year.

If you know a fan who deserves a Wolves Wish, please email wishes@wolves.co.uk.

THE
BEARDS
THAT ARE
FEARED

An ever-growing (literally) footballing fashion in recent years has been the number of players who have started sporting substantial beards. Wolves has been no exception, and perhaps none more than the legendary Jack Price, whose beard often appears to be taller than him.

We have decided to put together a team of best beards, in 4-4-2 formation, with our very own Pricey obviously included. Some pretty big name beards have missed out. But see what you think of our every own Bristles City!

1 Tim Howard
Tim Howard's beard is so immense it has its own Twitter page. Former Everton and USA international gloveman will prove a strong and stubbly last line of defence for our bearded wonders.

2 John Brayford
Became a cult hero during his time with Sheffield United, nickname of course - the Blades. Which he clearly has no use for given his substantial amount of facial fuzz!

3 Joe Ledley
Famous for his dance when Wales reached the summer's European Championships. But far more famous for a healthy beard which has stood the test of time. Rumour has it his beard helped him make a miraculous recovery from a broken leg to be fit for the summer's tournament in France. Shave it off? You've got to be Joe-king.

4 Jack Price
Ah Pricey. The legend. The Shropshire Pirlo. Fear the Beard. Has progressed all the way from Wolves Academy to the first team. And his beard is the stuff of Molineux folklore. Shaved it off when he scored his first Wolves goal against Watford. And lost all his strength as a result. Never again Pricey. Never again.

5 Alexei Lalas
Surely the fore-runner for all beards which have followed. The American international defender who is believed to have once housed a family of four in his magnificent chin barnet.

6 Nicolas Otamendi
Manchester City defender who plays in the same Argentina team as Messi. But messy is not the word for his beard. Check out the contours on that baby!

7 Adam Clayton
If sharing his name with the bass guitarist from legendary rock band U2 isn't enough, the Middlesbrough midfielder has given himself some added X-Factor with a tremendous specimen growing from his chin. Magnificent. Even Better Than The Real Thing. Adam has certainly 'found what he's looking for' with this beauty.

8 Andrea Pirlo
Andrea Pirlo. With a supreme beard. Nothing more to add Your Honour.

9 Davide Moscardelli
You say Moscardelli — we say 'What a beard'. The second part of the hairiest strike force ever seen is the experienced Belgian frontman currently with Lecce. Mutton Chops Moscardelli has to be his nickname in the Lecce dressing room.

10 Marco Sailer
Hello Sailer! What a 5 o'clock shadow on the German striker currently with SV Darmstadt 98. A flock of blackbirds was once seen departing the spectacular hair. Way to go Marco!

11 Stuart Dallas
Who shot JR? What happened to Bobby Ewing in the shower? Forget that Dallas. It's all about this Dallas. Stuart Dallas. A Northern Ireland winger whose beard is more than worthy of its own American TV series.

MATCH LINE-UP

1

2  **5**  **6**  **3**

7  **4**  **8**  **11**

10  **9**

PRICEY'S VERDICT!

"What a team that is. And what an honour to be selected in the centre of midfield. I don't know what it is with my beard – I just started growing it. And liked it!

I did shave it off as promised after the Watford goal but I don't think I'll be making 'rash' promises like that again.

The beard is here to stay. As is hopefully my place in this team of Best Beards! We'll certainly all be razor sharp."

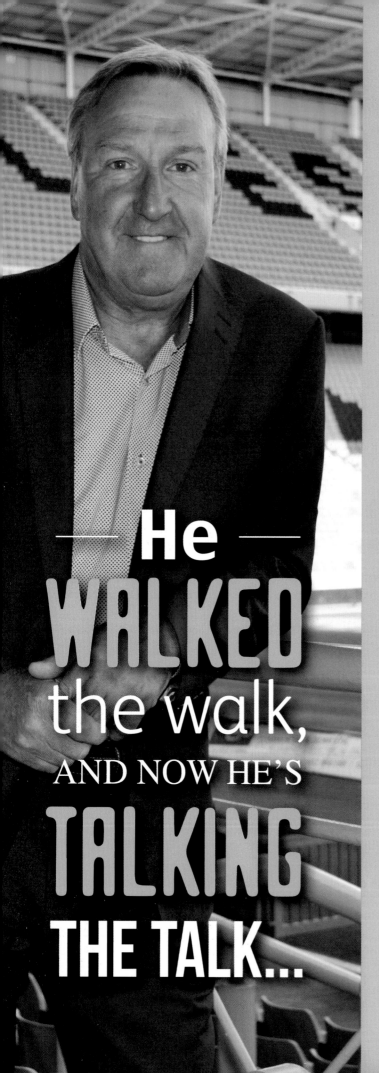

He
WALKED
the walk,
AND NOW HE'S
TALKING
THE TALK...

There are many former Wolves players who have retained strong links with the club since they finished playing, remained in the local area, and remained as popular as ever amongst those fans who used to cheer them from the stands.

Steve Daley is one such player, who has gone on to forge several different successful careers after hanging up his boots. Having left Wolves for Manchester City for an English record transfer fee in 1979, things didn't quite go according to plan. But Steve has used the tough experiences of his career as food for thought in a new role as a motivational speaker.

Back to the start first Steve, how did you first get spotted by Wolves?

I used to play for Cudworth West End Working Mens Club in the Barnsley & District Sunday League. And I was training with Wath Wanderers, Wolves' feeder team. I remember as though it was yesterday the Sunday morning when Wolves scout Mark Crook came to watch me. On the afternoon he spent two-and-a-half hours talking to my Mum and Dad to persuade them to let me come to Wolves, and on the Monday I was here.

It was a month's trial, which turned into three. I don't think anyone knew I was here! I was 15 at that point. Bill McGarry had just taken over as manager and a bit later on he called me into his office and told me I'd got a three year contract as an apprentice. And it went from there.

And how did it go from there? You had some great times at Wolves?

I made my first team debut in the 1971-72 season against Southampton and I scored in a 4-2 win. And that was great because I had also scored on my debut for the youth team, my debut for the reserves, debut for the first team, debut for England 'B', and debut in the UEFA Cup after 16 seconds against Ferencvaros. I'm not sure if that is still a record for the quickest goal in a European game. If someone else says they have done 11 then I'll change mine to 10!

And so many of you from that time are still really good friends today?

I was here with some great lads. The other two lads in the middle of the park that I played with for seasons were Kenny Hibbitt and Willie Carr. All three of us used to contribute a lot of goals. We'd got John Richards, Derek Dougan, Steve Kindon, Alan Sunderland up front. I remember the one season – 1976/77 I think – when we got promoted back to the top division and we were scoring goals for fun. It was amazing. It was great to play alongside all those guys and so many of us have stayed in touch. Lofty (Phil Parkes) unfortunately – only joking mate - and also Derek Parkin, John McAlle, Geoff Palmer, John Richards, Kindo, Mel Eves. We still all stick together and meet up every now and again and have a couple of beers or a game of golf. So many times I get told, 'I bet you wish you were playing today'. And to be honest, ask any of us Wolves lads from those days in the 1970s, and I don't think we would change it for the world. It was such a great time.

And then, when you were at the peak of your career, came Manchester City....

I was transferred in 1979 and you often look back at the mistakes you make in football. Leaving Wolves was the biggest mistake I ever made. I thought I was going to Manchester City to play with the likes of Gary Owen, Peter Barnes, Asa Hartford and Micky Channon. But when I'd got there they had all gone. I signed the longest contract in history I think, for ten years. And after 18 months I was off to America with Seattle Sounders. There were all sorts of things going on at City. I was getting death threats and different bits and pieces. I remember playing Halifax in a cup game at The Shay. They were bottom of the old Fourth Division, but they beat us 1-0. There was a knock on the door after the final whistle and it was the Yorkshire Chief of Police saying it

would be in the interests of Steve Daley to have a police escort from the dressing room to the coach. And Joe Corrigan, bless him, said the only people taking Steve out to the coach were his team-mates. I thanked him for his backing, and then told him he was the one who had conceded the goal! It just seemed easier because of everything that was going on at Manchester City to put the entire burden on one man's shoulders – and that was mine.

How did it all come to a head at City?

I remember one of my last games was at Brighton. I got sent off for nearly cutting John Gregory in two, which was totally out of character for me. After the game the referee knocked the door and asked to have a word. He took me out on the pitch and said he was ever so sorry for sending me off. I said I was sorry for putting him in that position. He said his proper job was in psychology and that when he'd looked at me while he was sending me off he was thinking 'what has happened to this kid, there is nothing there.' That turned it around for me. To be honest, at that time I was so desperate I had contemplated doing something stupid. He just said a few things that got through to me, that decisions were now being made for me which were wrong, rather than me making them like I had at Wolves. He suggested I went to play abroad, in a new environment with a new challenge. Within weeks I was on my way to Seattle Sounders which I loved. And then I came back to England for one last season at Walsall with Alan Buckley.

And then, at the end of your playing career?

After coming out of my comfort zone as professional footballer I have done various different things. I was a sales rep for Carlsberg Tetley, I now do a lot of after dinner speaking, some radio commentary, and motivational speaking as well. I'm busier now than I have ever been - and I am loving it.

Yes talk to us about the motivational speaking....

It has been going really well. I go out to colleges and academies, schools, and have been to the Academy at Wolves. It's really to say that whatever you want to achieve in your life, in any walk of life or industry, you can do it. I was a footballer for ten years at Wolves and, in total, 18 years. That wasn't because I was a great player, it was because I had a great determination and belief. You have to set yourself goals and targets to achieve over a period of time. I learned forward planning from my brother and my dad because my brother played for Sheffield Wednesday and my dad for Coventry. Far better players than me never made the grade. But I went for it, and I got there.

What sort of response do you get from the speaking?

I've had a good response.
I have recently been invited to Winson Green Prison to talk to the inmates with a view to travelling to prisons around the country. It is about positive thinking, by drawing on your strengths you can turn a negative into a positive. We all have the ability to improve our life - anything is possible.

Anyone who would like further details about Steve's motivational speaking or is interested in booking him should email stevedaley01@aol.com.

A KITMAN'S GUIDE!

There are many roles in the backroom staff at Wolves which go on behind the scenes to try and ensure everything is in place for the players. One of those is that of a kitman. Whether it's for training or matches, treatment or travelling to a game, all the players need to have the right kit and footwear.

We caught up with Wolves' kitman Steve Morton to pick up ten tips of the trade! So here's Morts' guide to being a kitman.

1 BE READY FOR LONG HOURS
It's not a 9 to 5 job, or a five day week. There are a lot of early mornings and late returns, especially after an evening away game. It can sometimes be a 4am finish after sorting the kit out after getting back.

2 BE A GOOD TRAVEL GUIDE
Knowing where all the stadiums are, keeping up to date with traffic on a matchday. You have to get the kit there in plenty of time whether travelling by coach or in our van.

3 BE FRIENDLY TO COACH DRIVERS
Important people to keep sweet. They can pick things up from Molineux for me if I am stuck at the training ground before leaving and drop me off at the stadium at the other end!

4 BE READY WITH THE BANTER
Give us as much as you take. Or the players will walk all over you. They are a good bunch here and enjoy it if you argue back!

5 BE A SHOULDER TO CRY ON
I sometimes feel like a 52-year-old Dad to about 20 people between the ages of 18 and a bit older! You often find yourself in a position where they might want to sound off about football and plenty more!

6 BE PREPARED FOR A POOR DIET
With the hours there is a lot of grabbing things on the run and eating rubbish. I suppose I should really compensate on other days. Fine figure of a man that I am. But there is nothing better than getting home after a match and finding the Chinese still open.

7 BE VERY ORGANISED
You have to know where everything is at the drop of a hat. If a player needs something urgently on a matchday you can't go around looking for it for 20 minutes. Getting the kit ready for a home game and in the dressing room usually starts on a Thursday afternoon before a Saturday game.

8 BE TRUSTWORTHY
Sometimes you get to hear confidential information, which needs to be kept quiet. And I will get the team in advance as I have to fill the teamsheet in for the match officials. It is about keeping that info quiet.

9 BE KNOWLEDGEABLE - ABOUT BOOTS
Players have so many different boots now, and trainers, for the matches and training sessions they do. It's all about knowing whose belong to whom and a lot of the same. And of course we have to keep them clean too.

10 BE FRIENDLY WITH THE STAFF
It's always important to get on well with the gaffer and all the staff and it helps the atmosphere at the club and with the players. I have a particularly lively relationship with Tony Daley with the banter flying both ways. Dales is super fit and healthy so it may just be that sometimes something far less healthy finds its way into his kit on a matchday.

THEY WORE
1877 THE SHIRT 2017

Celebrating 140 years of Wolverhampton Wanderers' iconic strip

Steve Plant is one of the many fans who was introduced to – and went on to love – everything associated with Wolves thanks to the passion and support of his Dad.

But Steve's Dad John, who sadly passed away after a lengthy battle with cancer in 2012, also provided the inspiration for another Wolves-related project which has now hit the bookshelves.

'They Wore The Shirt' is a glossy hardback publication which takes a look at Wolves' 140-year history to date via the medium of 113 of the club's shirts, in 256 carefully-crafted pages.

Mr Plant senior first took Steve and brother Simon to a Wolves match in 1969 – a 0-0 draw against Manchester United at Molineux. Simon went on to support United, whilst Steve plumped for Wolves, leading to many contrasting fortunes being discussed at family gatherings down the years!

Steve's passion for Wolves developed into following the team home and away, and also running a coach for Hatherton Wolves for fans from the Kingswinford, Wordsley and Stourbridge areas.

One week they arranged a diversion to pick up George and Joan Bull from Tipton, parents to a certain Stephen George Bull, and the start of a friendship which saw Steve (Plant) regularly take Bully's parents to Wolves and England fixtures, coming into contact with the likes of Bobby Robson and Paul Gascoigne as a result. At that stage however Steve hadn't developed his interest in memorabilia – as he explains, that was to follow later.

"It was in 2009 that my Dad was diagnosed with cancer, which came right out of the blue."

A great **Christmas present** for the Wolves fan in your life!

With photography from Dave, Sam and Ed Bagnall, and extensive words accompanying the pictures from esteemed journalist David Instone, and plenty of input from Steve himself, the high-quality publication - which also features the names of sponsors and subscribers - is a real treasure trove for anyone interested not just in memorabilia but also the history of Wolves.

Designed by Synaxis Design Consultancy Ltd, this excellent publication retails at £25 (plus £5 P&P if unable to pick up from Molineux).

"He didn't want any treatment, he said he had enjoyed a great life and wanted the treatment to be concentrated on someone younger with their whole lives ahead of them. He went downhill pretty quickly, and was only given three months to live. At the time, I brought a George Elokobi matchworn shirt on Ebay for £50, complete with a hole in it and Vic stain in the middle! It was something to try and interest my Dad and when I showed him he perked up a bit, so I decided to get some more, set up a memorabilia website and get my Dad a laptop so he could keep an eye on the progress. He started taking a real interest in it, I think it really helped him, and when he eventually passed away in 2012, he had

beaten his expected diagnosis by three years. Towards the end, there was a time when I was nursing him to give my Mum a break, and he told me how chuffed he had been with what I had done with the shirts. We talked about doing a book, and he told me to go for it, and now I am finally in a position where I think we have done it justice. Neil Taylor is a good friend of mine, and he has raised a fantastic amount for Birmingham Children's Hospital, who have looked after his daughter Kiahna. With that, and my Dad wanting to support a cancer charity, all the proceeds from the book will go to Birmingham Children's Hospital."

 Follow @thewolvesshirt on Twitter or email wolvesandengland@hotmail.co.uk for details.

 supporting Birmingham Children's Hospital

EDDO'S
INCREDIBLE
JOURNEY

Wales not only took part in
their first major tournament for
58 years in France this summer,
they also made it all the way to the
semi finals, before a 2-0 defeat to
Portugal ended their Euro 2016 adventure.

Wolves midfielder Dave Edwards was
delighted to be a part of it, as he
completed a quickfire recovery from
injury to make it into the final squad.

DID YOU KNOW?

Eddo featured in all three of Wales's group games, starting the win against Slovakia and coming off the bench against England and Russia.

The game against England saw Eddo up against his former tenant – keeper Joe Hart – the pair having shared a house during their time at Shrewsbury Town.

Eddo was joined by two former Wolves players in the Welsh squad, keeper Wayne Hennessey and striker Sam Vokes, whilst head physio Sean Connolly also played for the club.

After the Northern Ireland fixture, Eddo was delighted to welcome his children Jack and Evie onto the pitch for an impromptu kick about!

With an average of 1.67 goals per game, Wales had the third highest ratio in the tournament, behind only France and Belgium, whom they beat in the quarter finals.

Eddo's Player of the Tournament was his Welsh team-mate Gareth Bale, who scored three goals in the competition.

There were 73 days between Edwards breaking his metatarsal against QPR and returning to action against MK Dons, helping him book his place in the tournament.

Eddo made his Wales debut in November 2007, coming off the bench to replace former Wolves midfielder Carl Robinson in a European Championships qualifier against the Republic of Ireland.

EDDO SAYS:

"It was an amazing seven weeks, and I wouldn't change it for the world.

It is incredible to think what it meant to the people of Wales."

Young Wolves
Membership

From being served by the Wolves players in Nando's, to watching them in action at an Open Training Session, or getting up close and personal for autographs and selfies at the Christmas and End of Season parties, it is always a busy time for the members of Young Wolves!

Here are a few pictorial memories of another exciting Young Wolves season!

Be Part of the #WolvesFamily
#PassItOn

Join **Young Wolves** or **#WolfPack** junior membership for season 2016/17 today.

Ages **4-11**

Ages **12-16**

JUST **£20**

Young Wolves

JUST **£20**

 # Wolf Pack

Members receive Souvenir tin, photo frame, note pad and torch pen.

Members receive Souvenir tin, I touch gloves, scarf and keyring.

We love having you in the **#WolvesFamily**. **#PassItOn** to the next generation.

For £20, memberships include:

- Exclusive members only joining gift

- **NEW FOR 2016/17** Free ticket to 3 matches of your choice (Excludes Bristol City, QPR, Villa, Newcastle & Preston North End)

- Members only draw to win the chance to be an away mascot

- Earn cash rewards on tickets and merchandise

- Members receive exclusive offers from our partners – Nando's and Grand Theatre

- All members will receive a personalised smartcard

- Priority on league, cup and play-off match tickets

- Special events, including the Christmas Party

Buy online at **wolvesmembership.co.uk**
or call the Ticket Office on **0871 222 1877**.

MAKE A DATE!

Another quiz now, and this time it's about placing a match or Wolves-related event to a month in the year.

We have gone back over the last decade and found 12 notable Wolves-related games or landmarks which took place in different months of the year. Simply match the event to the month – January to December! It's a tricky one – and may take some working out!

An emotional day at Molineux

as Wolves join together to pay tribute to Sir Jack Hayward, and late goals from Dave Edwards and Benik Afobe seal a 2-0 win against Blackpool.

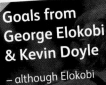

Goals from George Elokobi & Kevin Doyle

– although Elokobi wanted to claim both! – secure Wolves a famous home win and end Manchester United's 29-game league unbeaten run.

Jody Craddock

later to be awarded a testimonial, makes his last Wolves appearance, poetically against his previous club as a Steven Fletcher double helps account for Sunderland 2-1.

An event to celebrate the future

as Wolves mark the official opening of the new £7million Academy Arena at their Compton Park training complex.

Wolves play two games

on a fortnight's pre-season tour of Australia, ahead of the return to the Premier League in the 2009/10 season.

An incredible game at Molineux

featuring 10 goals, as already promoted Wolves defeat Rotherham 6-4.

Sylvan Ebanks-Blake

chalks up his 50th league goal for Wolves, in a 2-0 win away at Peterborough.

A hugely impressive 4-1 win

at Swindon and Kenny Jackett's Wolves break a long-standing club record – posting nine successive victories.

One of those truly magical Molineux afternoons

as a Wolves team already promoted to the Premier League beat Doncaster 1-0 thanks to Richard Stearman's late header.

A lunchtime 0-0 draw

at Villa Park makes for a superb start to Wolves' Premier League season, seven points from three games taking the team – only for a few hours – top of the division.

Wolves preparing for a return

to the Premier League, break their club record with the signing of striker Kevin Doyle from Reading.

A fun-filled Sunday

spent at Molineux as popular keeper Matt Murray enjoys his testimonial with a fixture between a Matt Murray XI and an All Stars XI.

MY GUESSES:

Answers on page **61**

1. _____
2. _____
3. _____
4. _____
5. _____
6. _____

7. _____
8. _____
9. _____
10. _____
11. _____
12. _____

GOING FOR
GOLD!

Wolves fan Kristian Thomas has progressed a long way from his days at school next door to the Compton Park training ground. Kristian has reached the very top of his sport – gymnastics – and was part of a history-making team effort at the London 2012 Olympics.

More recently, he could also be seen in action in individual and team events at Rio 2016.

We caught up with him to find out more about his career so far, and – of course – his support of **Wolves**!

What school did you go to and were you a good student?

I went to St. Edmund's Catholic Academy which is on Compton Park right next to the Wolves training ground. I think on the whole, I was a good student and always enjoyed my time at St Edmund's. However, now I know I can't get in trouble for it, there might have been a few occasions where I used the excuse I was at morning training and instead I was late because I just wanted a lie-in!

What sports did you do at school and when did you start to get really serious with the gymnastics?

At school I pretty much did all sports. Though football, athletics and swimming were the main ones I enjoyed. PE was always my favourite subject, so I was willing to give any sport a good go. Gymnastics started getting serious around the age of 15 when I was asked to compete in my first competition for Great Britain. From the age of 12, I had been training around 20 plus hours a week, but this was my first opportunity to compete internationally. When I returned to school after my first international, I told my friends how we finished 4th. However, what I chose not to tell them was that there were only four countries competing!

When did you make your big breakthrough in international competition?

My big break came through at 17 years old when I was selected to represent England in 2006 at the Commonwealth Games in Melbourne in Australia. Though I was only a junior competing against people much older then me, we came away with a team bronze medal and I knew from that moment standing on the podium that I wanted to continue competing at the highest level and become a full time athlete.

The London Olympics – and an historic bronze medal in the team event. What was that time like and how do you sum up the achievement?

To put it simply, the London Olympics was just an incredible experience. There was a lot of negative media initially surrounding the Games, but once the Opening Ceremony started and the medals started to come through, then I think it's fair to say that the nation got behind all of the Team GB athletes and helped fuel them to more success. Winning an Olympic bronze medal made all the sacrifices and commitments well worth it, and doing it in front of a home crowd made it even more special. The support that we received during those games was amazing and it remains without a doubt the highlight of my career to date.

Sitting next to the Duchess of Cambridge during the Olympics – how did that come about and what was she chatting about?!

I was just in the right place at the right time I guess, because still to this day I've got no idea how I was chosen to sit next to her. She was very easy to talk to and asked questions relating to gymnastics and what to look out for. In particular, the Pommel Horse, being as we were watching my team mates win Olympic Silver and Bronze on the Pommel Horse that day.

And since those Olympics you have also enjoyed more successes?

The results from the 2012 Olympics encouraged me and gave me the confidence to continue competing at the highest level, and since then I've gone on to win two World Championship Medals in 2013 and 2105 (bronze on vault, silver in the team) five European medals including becoming European Champion on floor in 2015, and three Commonwealth Games Medals - including a team gold -in 2014.

How do you prepare on the day of the competition? Do you get nervous?

I like to start the day of competition off with scrambled eggs and baked beans, with of course brown sauce. This is my lucky breakfast meal and sets me up for the day. Generally on competition days there will always be nerves but I try to take my focus away from gymnastics by watching a film, reading, or listening to slower paced chilled out music. These all help to keep me relaxed.

Changing the subject to Wolves, how long have you supported the club and do you get to many matches?

Having been born in Wednesfield in Wolverhampton I've always supported Wolves. Growing up, I wasn't able to get to many matches due to always training on the weekends but I think my first ever Wolves game was against Bury FC when I was about 8. Now that my training schedule is a bit more flexible i'm able to come to a lot more Wolves games and show my support.

Any favourite Wolves memory so far?

It has got to be the 2003 play off final against Sheffield United. Though I wasn't able to get to the game I remember watching it, and remember how much of a high the city of Wolverhampton was on, especially for the parade a few days later.

And finally, based on your achievements in your career so far, what one piece of advice would you give to young people in terms of what they want to achieve?

The best advice I can give to younger people is, don't be afraid to dream big. Anybody with the right grit and determination can be successful in their chosen field, and it takes a lot of hard work, dedication and commitment, but the rewards are well worth it.

Follow Kristian on Twitter @kristian_thomas

PLAYER PROFILES

KEEPING IT REAL!

Jon **FLATT**

Carl **IKEME**

Andy **LONERGAN**

CASE FOR THE DEFENCE

Cameron **BORTHWICK-JACKSON**

Richard **STEARMAN**

Dominic **IORFA**

Kortney **HAUSE**

Matt **DOHERTY**

Ethan **EBANKS-LANDELL**

Sylvain **DESLANDES**

Danny **BATTH**

Mike **WILLIAMSON**

Silvio **SA PEREIRA**

MIDFIELD MAESTROS

Conor **COADY**

Joao **TEIXEIRA**

Jack **PRICE**

Lee **EVANS**

George **SAVILLE**

Dave **EDWARDS**

Jed **WALLACE**

Romain **SAISS**

Jordan **GRAHAM**

Prince **ONIANGUE**

THE FORWARD THINKERS

Ivan **CAVALEIRO**

Paul **GLADON**

Jon Dadi **BODVARSSON**

Michal **ZYRO**

James **HENRY**

Nouha **DICKO**

Joe **MASON**

Helder **COSTA**

Bright **ENOBAKHARE**

Ola **JOHN**

NICE PIECE OF KIT!

Here they are, all Wolves' replica kit for the 2016/17 season, including something of a retro return to pinstripes for the home shirt for the first time since the 1980s.

All kits, as well as Wolves' range of training wear for the current campaign, are available online or from the Wolves megastores at Molineux and Dudley Street.

THE ANSWERS...

Page 22:

GETTING SHIRTY!

DICKO   SAVILLE   EDWARDS

SPOT THE DIFFERENCE

CREST JUMBLE

BRISTOL CITY   QPR   BURTON ALBION   NORWICH CITY

PUZZLED!

Page 23:

MONSTER WORDSEARCH

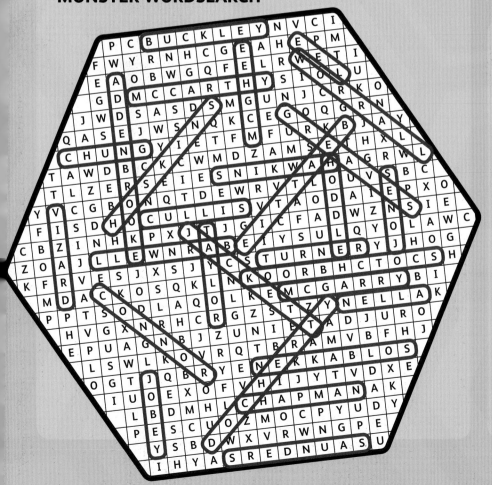

Pages 52 & 53:

MAKE A DATE!

1. APRIL

2. SEPTEMBER

3. JANUARY

4. MARCH

5. MAY

6. FEBRUARY

7. DECEMBER

8. AUGUST

9. JUNE

10. NOVEMBER

11. JULY

12. OCTOBER

Where's Wolfie?

Wolfie is hidden amongst the Wolves fans! Can you find him?